Delicious
snacks

Delicious
snacks

Love Food ™ is an imprint of Parragon Books Ltd

Parragon
Queen Street House
4 Queen Street
Bath BA1 1HE, UK

Cover and internal design by Mark Cavanagh
Introduction by Bridget Jones
Photography by Günter Beer
Additional photography by Clive Bozzard-Hill, Karen Thomas and Laurie Evans
Home Economists Stevan Paul, Sandra Baddeley, Sue Henderson, Valerie Berry, Annie Rigg and Philippa Vanstone

ISBN 978-1-4054-9272-0
Printed in China

Notes for the reader
• This book uses imperial, metric, and US cup measurements. Follow the same units of measurement throughout; do not mix imperial and metric.
• All spoon measurements are level: teaspoons are assumed to be 5 ml, and tablespoons are assumed to be 15 ml.
• Unless otherwise stated, milk is assumed to be lowfat and eggs are medium. The times given are an approximate guide only.
• Some recipes contain nuts. If you are allergic to nuts you should avoid using them and any products containing nuts. Recipes using raw or very lightly cooked eggs should be avoided by infants, the elderly, pregnant women, convalescents, and anyone suffering from illness.

Contents

Snacks

Juggling duty and desire is part of the modern lifestyle, and the way we eat matches our kaleidoscope of commitments. Many people work away from home and each day is not necessarily identical to the last. There are frequent days when family members are busy with separate activities and need to eat at different times. It is therefore not always easy to plan for, prepare, and eat formal meals. Eating small amounts frequently fits busy lifestyles—breakfasts on the go, mid-morning snacks, packed lunches, after-work snacks, and late, but light, suppers are typical eating occasions.

Social snacking

From a casual buffet to a formal canapé party, festive gatherings are classic snacking occasions. When feeding a crowd, two or three homemade items will transform a basic selection of nuts, chips, crackers, and other bought snacks, making them more interesting and substantial.

Here are some tips to make entertaining easy:
• The best party snacks can be prepared ahead and cooked at the last minute with minimum fuss, or served cold.
• Fit the presentation to the occasion—snacks lined up on platters with stylish garnishes look impressive.
• Instead of plates, have bright paper napkins to wipe sticky fingers.
• Put out bowls where guests can deposit discarded toothpicks.
• Stagger snacks during a party, handing out alternating trays of different types.

Minimum effort: maximum flavor

Take-out food tends to be full of fat, misses out on good nutrients, and comes in portion sizes that make us eat more than we need. The TV Snacks chapter has recipes that are the right compromise for times when slaving

over a hot stove is not an option. Unlike their bought counterparts, these are free from artificial additives, and are fresh and delicious. Oven-fried Chicken Wings, Homemade Oven Fries, and Classic Spare Ribs need minimum attention once they're in the oven. Add a bag of prepared salad and follow with some fresh fruit for a vitamin boost.

Light lunches or late nights

Lighter eating is good when working late, socializing early evening, or providing a cab service for children's out-of-school activities. It's often late evening before there's a chance to sit and eat, and satisfying but light dishes are best. Eating light occasionally is also good for keeping weight in check. Spicy Shrimp, Parma Ham with Melon & Asparagus, or Red Cabbage Slaw are good examples of suitable dishes. Keep breads in the freezer, ready cut for thawing in the microwave—ciabatta, bagels, crusty French, or light rye make light dishes

more substantial. Instant couscous can be ready in minutes to complement light dishes without making them too heavy.

Eating out and about

Here are a few reminders for practical packed lunches:
• Use insulated containers and/or bags and drink holders to keep food fresh. They come in all sizes, from individual pots to picnic baskets for a feast.
• For warming drinks or soups, small vacuum flasks are ideal. Insulated pots are good for chunky soups or stews.
• Fresh fruit and/or salad or raw vegetable sticks are vital in daily packed lunches. For salads on the go, make sure to pack dressings in a screw-top jar and add them at the last minute to keep salad greens crisp.
• Try cook-ahead foods for a meal one day and packed lunch the next: make Spanish Omelet for supper, and chill some for a packed lunch. Soups and sushi can also be prepared ahead.

1

Mouthwatering Morsels

serves 4

3 skinless, boneless chicken breasts

4 tbsp whole wheat flour

1 tbsp wheat germ

$\frac{1}{2}$ tsp ground cumin

$\frac{1}{2}$ tsp ground coriander

pepper

1 egg, lightly beaten

2 tbsp olive oil

green salad, to serve

for the dipping sauce

$3\frac{1}{2}$ oz/100 g roasted cherry tomatoes

$3\frac{1}{2}$ oz/100 g fresh tomatoes, peeled, seeded, and chopped

2 tbsp mayonnaise

chicken nuggets

Preheat the oven to 375°F/190°C. Cut the chicken breasts into $1\frac{1}{2}$-inch/4-cm chunks. Mix the flour, wheat germ, cumin, coriander, and pepper to taste in a bowl, then divide in half and put on 2 separate plates. Put the beaten egg on a third plate.

Pour the oil into a baking sheet with a rim and heat in the oven. Roll the chicken pieces in one plate of flour, shake to remove any excess, then roll in the egg and in the second plate of flour, again shaking off any excess flour. When all the nuggets are ready, remove the baking sheet from the oven and toss the nuggets in the hot oil. Roast in the oven for 25–30 minutes until golden and crisp.

Meanwhile, to make the dipping sauce, put both kinds of tomatoes in a blender or food processor and process until smooth. Add the mayonnaise and process again until well combined.

Remove the nuggets from the oven and drain on paper towels. Serve with the dipping sauce and a green salad.

serves 4

4 oz/115 g sirloin or rump steak

4 white mushrooms, cut into $1/2$-inch/1-cm cubes

$1/2$ small onion, cut into $1/2$-inch/1-cm cubes

for the spicy tomato marinade

$1/4$ cup tomato juice

$1/4$ cup beef stock

1 tbsp Worcestershire sauce

1 tbsp lemon juice

2 tbsp dry sherry

few drops of Tabasco sauce

2 tbsp vegetable oil

1 tbsp minced celery

miniature beef kabobs

Cut the steak into $1/2$-inch/1-cm cubes. Combine all the marinade ingredients in a large, nonmetallic bowl, whisk well and stir in the meat, mushrooms, and onion. Cover with plastic wrap and let marinate in the refrigerator for 30 minutes.

Drain off the marinade and set aside. Place alternating pieces of steak and vegetables on toothpicks, taking care not to pack them together too tightly.

Preheat a griddle pan or heavy-bottom skillet over high heat. Place the kabobs in the pan and cook, turning frequently, for 5 minutes, or until gently browned and cooked through.

Pile the kabobs high on platters and serve at once.

serves 4

1 lb/450 g lean, finely ground lamb

1 medium onion

1 garlic clove, crushed

1/2 cup fresh white or brown breadcrumbs

1 tbsp chopped fresh mint

1 tbsp chopped fresh parsley

salt and pepper

1 egg, beaten

olive oil, for brushing

warm pita bread and salad, to serve

grecian meatballs

Put the ground lamb in a bowl. Grate in the onion, then add the garlic, breadcrumbs, mint, and parsley. Season well with salt and pepper. Mix the ingredients well then add the beaten egg and mix to bind the mixture together. Alternatively, the ingredients can be mixed in a food processor.

With damp hands, form the mixture into 16 small balls and thread onto 4 flat metal skewers. Lightly oil a broiler pan and brush the meatballs with oil.

Preheat the broiler to medium and cook the meatballs for 10 minutes, turning frequently, and brushing with more oil if necessary, until browned. Serve the meatballs tucked into warm pita bread with salad.

serves 2

6 tbsp mayonnaise

2 garlic cloves, crushed

2 large whitefish fillets, skinned

1 egg, beaten

3 heaping tbsp whole wheat flour

vegetable oil, for deep-frying

lemon wedges, to garnish

fish goujons with garlic mayonnaise

Combine the mayonnaise and garlic in a small dish. Cover with plastic wrap and refrigerate while you cook the fish.

Cut the fish into 1-inch/2.5-cm strips. Dip the strips in the egg, then drain and dredge in flour. Meanwhile, heat the oil in a deep-fryer or large saucepan to 350–375°F/180–190°C, or until a cube of bread browns in 30 seconds.

Fry the pieces of fish in the hot oil for 3–4 minutes, or until golden brown. Remove from the oil and drain on a dish lined with paper towels.

Remove the garlic mayonnaise from the refrigerator and stir once. Serve the fish on an attractive dish, garnished with lemon wedges, with the mayonnaise on the side for dipping.

makes 20

7 oz/200 g canned tuna in spring water, drained

1 egg, beaten

1 tsp minced fresh parsley

sea salt and pepper

scant 1 cup fresh whole wheat breadcrumbs

about 1 tbsp whole wheat flour

vegetable oil, for brushing

tuna bites

Mash the tuna with the egg, parsley, a pinch of salt, and pepper to taste. Add the breadcrumbs and mix well, then add enough of the flour to bind the mixture together.

Divide the mixture into 20 mini portions, shape each portion into a ball, and let chill for 15 minutes.

Meanwhile, preheat the oven to 375°F/190°C. Brush a nonstick baking sheet with a little oil. Space the tuna balls out on the baking sheet and brush with a little more oil. Bake in the preheated oven for 15–20 minutes until golden and crisp.

Remove from the oven and drain on paper towels. Serve warm or cold.

serves 4

1 1/3 cups dried chickpeas

1 large onion, finely chopped

1 garlic clove, crushed

2 tbsp chopped fresh parsley, plus extra sprigs to garnish

2 tsp ground cumin

2 tsp ground coriander

1/2 tsp baking powder

cayenne pepper

salt

oil, for deep-frying

to serve

hummus (see page 84)

tomato wedges

pita bread

falafel

Soak the chickpeas overnight in enough cold water to cover them and allow room for expansion. Drain, then place in a pan, cover with fresh water, and bring to a boil. Reduce the heat and let simmer for 1 hour, or until tender. Drain.

Place the chickpeas in a food processor and blend to make a coarse paste. Add the onion, garlic, parsley, cumin, coriander, baking powder, and cayenne pepper and salt to taste. Blend again to mix thoroughly.

Cover and let rest for 30 minutes, then shape into 8 balls. Let rest for an additional 30 minutes. Heat the oil in a wok or large pan to 350–375°F/180–190°C, or until a cube of bread browns in 30 seconds. Gently drop in the balls and cook until golden brown. Remove from the oil and drain on a plate lined with paper towels.

Serve hot or at room temperature with hummus, tomato wedges, and pita bread. Garnish with sprigs of parsley.

serves 4

4 oz/115 g fresh white bread

2 tbsp freshly grated
Parmesan cheese

1 tsp paprika

2 egg whites

8 oz/225 g white mushrooms

for the aïoli

4 garlic cloves, crushed

salt and pepper

2 egg yolks

1 cup extra virgin olive oil

mushroom bites with aïoli

Preheat the oven to 375°F/190°C. To make the aïoli, put the garlic in a bowl, add a pinch of salt, and mash with the back of a spoon. Add the egg yolks and beat with an electric mixer for 30 seconds, or until creamy. Start beating in the oil, one drop at a time. As the mixture starts to thicken, add the oil in a steady stream, beating constantly. Season to taste with salt and pepper, cover the bowl with plastic wrap, and let chill in the refrigerator until required.

Line a large baking sheet with parchment paper. Grate the bread into breadcrumbs and place them in a bowl with the Parmesan cheese and paprika. Lightly whisk the egg whites in a separate clean bowl, then dip each mushroom first into the egg whites, then into the breadcrumbs, and place on the prepared baking sheet.

Bake in the preheated oven for 15 minutes, or until the coating is crisp and golden. Serve at once with the aïoli.

serves 8

4 garlic cloves, peeled

2 tsp coriander seeds

1 small lemon

1 lb/450 g canned or bottled large green pitted olives, drained

4 fresh thyme sprigs

4 feathery stalks of fennel

2 small fresh red chiles (optional)

pepper

extra virgin olive oil

spicy marinated olives

Using the flat side of a broad knife, lightly crush each garlic clove. Using a mortar and pestle, crack the coriander seeds. Cut the lemon, with its rind, into small chunks.

Place the olives, garlic, coriander seeds, lemon chunks, thyme sprigs, fennel, and chiles, if using, in a large bowl and toss together. Season to taste with pepper, but you should not need to add salt as canned or bottled olives are usually salty enough. Pack the ingredients tightly into a glass jar with a lid. Pour in enough olive oil to cover the olives, then seal the jar tightly.

Let the olives stand at room temperature for 24 hours, then marinate in the refrigerator for at least 1 week but preferably 2 weeks before serving. From time to time, gently give the jar a shake to re-mix the ingredients. Return the olives to room temperature and remove from the oil to serve. Provide wooden toothpicks for spearing the olives.

serves 4

corn oil, for deep-frying

1 large egg

pinch of salt

3/4 cup water

3/8 cup all-purpose flour

2 tsp ground cinnamon

generous 1/4 cup superfine sugar

4 apples, peeled and cored

apple fritters

Pour the corn oil into a deep fryer or large, heavy-bottom pan and heat to 350–375°F/180–190°C, or until a cube of bread browns in 30 seconds.

Meanwhile, using an electric mixer, beat the egg and salt together until frothy, then quickly whisk in the water and flour. Do not overbeat the batter—it doesn't matter if it isn't completely smooth.

Mix the cinnamon and sugar together in a shallow dish and set aside.

Slice the apples into 1/4-inch/5-mm thick rings. Spear with a fork, 1 slice at a time, and dip in the batter to coat. Add to the hot oil, in batches, and cook for 1 minute on each side, or until golden and puffed up. Remove with a slotted spoon and drain on paper towels. Keep warm while you cook the remaining batches. Transfer to a large serving plate, sprinkle with the cinnamon sugar, and serve.

serves 6

2^1/$_2$ cups good-quality
ice cream

7 oz/200 g semisweet chocolate

2 tbsp unsalted butter

chocolate ice-cream bites

Line a cookie sheet with plastic wrap.

Using a melon baller, scoop out balls of ice cream and place them on the prepared cookie sheet. Alternatively, cut the ice cream into bite-size cubes. Stick a toothpick in each piece and return to the freezer until very hard.

Place the chocolate and the butter in a heatproof bowl set over a pan of gently simmering water until melted. Quickly dip the frozen ice-cream balls into the warm chocolate and return to the freezer. Keep them there until ready to serve.

TV Snacks

makes 8

4 English muffins

1/2 cup prepared tomato
pizza sauce

2 sun-dried tomatoes in oil,
chopped

2 oz/55 g Parma ham

2 rings canned pineapple,
chopped

1/2 green bell pepper, seeded
and chopped

41/2 oz/125 g mozzarella
cheese, cubed

olive oil, for drizzling

salt and pepper

fresh basil leaves, to garnish

miniature ham & pineapple pizzas

Preheat the broiler to medium. Cut the English muffins in half
and toast the cut side lightly.

Spread the tomato sauce evenly over the English muffins.
Sprinkle the sun-dried tomatoes on top of the tomato sauce.
Cut the Parma ham into thin strips and place on the English
muffins with the pineapple and bell pepper. Carefully arrange
the mozzarella cubes on top. Drizzle a little oil over each pizza
and add salt and pepper to taste. Place under the hot broiler
and cook until the cheese melts and bubbles. Serve at once,
garnished with basil leaves.

serves 4

2 lb/900 g pork spare ribs

2 tbsp dark soy sauce

3 tbsp hoisin sauce

1 tbsp Chinese rice wine or dry sherry

pinch of Chinese five spice powder

2 tsp dark brown sugar

1/4 tsp chili sauce

2 garlic cloves, crushed

coriander sprigs, to garnish

classic spare ribs

Cut the spare ribs into separate pieces if they are joined together. If desired, you can chop them into 2-inch/5 cm lengths, using a cleaver.

Mix together the soy sauce, hoisin sauce, Chinese rice wine or sherry, Chinese five spice powder, dark brown sugar, chili sauce, and garlic in a large bowl.

Place the ribs in a shallow dish and pour the mixture over them, turning to coat them well. Cover and marinate in the refrigerator, turning the ribs from time to time, for at least 1 hour.

Remove the ribs from the marinade and arrange them in a single layer on a wire rack placed over a roasting pan half filled with warm water. Brush with the marinade, reserving the remainder.

Cook in a preheated oven, at 350°F/180°C, for 30 minutes. Remove the roasting pan from the oven and turn the ribs over. Brush with the remaining marinade and return to the oven for a further 30 minutes, or until cooked through. Transfer to a warmed serving dish, garnish with the coriander sprigs and serve immediately.

serves 4

2 tbsp vegetable or peanut oil

1 tbsp sesame oil

juice of 1/2 lime

2 skinless, boneless chicken breasts, cut into small cubes

for the dip

2 tbsp vegetable or peanut oil

1 small onion, chopped finely

1 small fresh green chile, seeded and chopped

1 garlic clove, chopped finely

1/2 cup crunchy peanut butter

6–8 tbsp water

juice of 1/2 lime

crushed peanuts, to garnish

chicken satay

Combine both the oils and the lime juice in a nonmetallic dish. Add the chicken cubes, cover with plastic wrap, and let chill for 1 hour.

To make the dip, heat the oil in a skillet and sauté the onion, chile, and garlic over low heat, stirring occasionally, for about 5 minutes, until just softened. Add the peanut butter, water, and lime juice and let simmer gently, stirring constantly, until the peanut butter has softened enough to make a dip—you may need to add extra water to make a thinner consistency.

Meanwhile, drain the chicken cubes and thread them onto 8–12 presoaked wooden skewers. Put under a hot broiler or on a barbecue, turning frequently, for about 10 minutes, until cooked and browned. Serve hot with the warm dip, garnished with crushed peanuts.

serves 4

12 chicken wings

1 egg

1/2 cup milk

4 heaping tbsp all-purpose flour

1 tsp paprika

salt and pepper

2 cups breadcrumbs

2 oz/55 g butter

oven-fried chicken wings

Preheat the oven to 425°F/220°C. Separate the chicken wings into 3 pieces each. Discard the bony tip. Beat the egg with the milk in a shallow dish. Combine the flour, paprika, and salt and pepper to taste in a separate shallow dish. Place the breadcrumbs in another shallow dish.

Dip the chicken pieces into the egg to coat well, then drain and roll in the seasoned flour. Remove, shaking off any excess, and roll the chicken in the breadcrumbs, gently pressing them onto the surface, then shaking off any excess.

Melt the butter in the preheated oven in a shallow roasting pan large enough to hold all the chicken pieces in a single layer. Arrange the chicken, skin-side down, in the pan and bake in the oven for 10 minutes. Turn and bake for an additional 10 minutes, or until the chicken is tender and the juices run clear when a skewer is inserted into the thickest part of the meat.

Remove the chicken from the pan and arrange on a large platter. Serve hot or at room temperature.

serves 6

14 oz/400 g canned white crabmeat

1–2 Thai chiles, to taste, seeded and finely chopped

6 scallions, finely shredded

1 zucchini, grated

1 carrot, grated

1 small yellow bell pepper, seeded and finely shredded

1/2 cup fresh bean sprouts, rinsed

1 tbsp chopped cilantro

1 large egg white

1–2 tbsp sunflower oil

for the salsa

1 Thai chile, seeded and finely chopped

2-inch/5-cm piece cucumber, grated

1 tbsp chopped cilantro

1 tbsp lime juice

1 tbsp Thai sweet chile sauce

1 tbsp peanuts, finely chopped (optional)

thai-style fish cakes

Mix all the fish cake ingredients, except for the egg white and oil, together. Whisk the egg white until frothy and just beginning to stiffen, then stir into the crab mixture. Then, using your hands, press about 1–2 tablespoons of the mixture together to form a fish cake. Repeat until 12 fish cakes are formed.

Make the salsa by combining all the ingredients except for the peanuts. Spoon into a small bowl, then cover and let stand for 30 minutes for the flavors to develop. Sprinkle with the peanuts, if using.

Heat 1 teaspoon of the oil in a nonstick skillet over low heat. Cook the fish cakes in batches for 2 minutes on each side over medium heat until lightly browned. Take care when turning them over. Remove and drain on paper towels. Repeat until all the fish cakes are cooked, using more oil if necessary. Serve immediately with the salsa.

serves 6

6 oz/175 g tortilla chips

14 oz/400 g canned refried
beans, warmed

2 tbsp finely chopped jarred
jalapeño chiles

7 oz/200 g canned or jarred
pimentos or roasted bell
peppers, drained and
finely sliced

salt and pepper

4 oz/115 g Gruyère cheese,
grated

4 oz/115 g Cheddar cheese,
grated

nachos

Preheat the oven to 400°F/200°C.

Spread the tortilla chips out over the bottom of a large, shallow, ovenproof dish or roasting pan. Cover with the warmed refried beans. Sprinkle over the chiles and pimentos and season to taste with salt and pepper. Mix the cheeses together in a bowl and sprinkle on top.

Bake in the preheated oven for 5–8 minutes, or until the cheese is bubbling and melted. Serve at once.

serves 4

2/3 cup long-grain rice

3 eggs, beaten

2 tbsp vegetable oil

2 garlic cloves, crushed

4 scallions, chopped

1 cup cooked peas

1 tbsp light soy sauce

pinch of salt

shredded scallion, to garnish

egg fried rice

Cook the rice in a pan of boiling water for 10–12 minutes, until almost cooked, but not soft. Drain well, rinse under cold water and drain again.

Place the beaten eggs in a nonstick saucepan and cook over a gentle heat, stirring until softly scrambled.

Heat the vegetable oil in a preheated wok or large skillet, swirling the oil around the base of the wok until it is really hot.

Add the crushed garlic, scallions, and peas and sauté, stirring occasionally, for 1–2 minutes. Stir the rice into the wok, mixing to combine.

Add the eggs, light soy sauce, and a pinch of salt to the wok or skillet and stir to mix the egg in thoroughly.

Transfer the egg fried rice to serving dishes and serve garnished with the shredded scallion.

serves 4

4 x 8 oz/225 g baking potatoes

2 tsp olive oil

coarse sea salt and pepper

for the guacamole dip

6 oz/175 g ripe avocado

1 tbsp lemon juice

2 ripe, firm tomatoes, chopped finely

1 tsp grated lemon rind

3 1/2 oz/100 g lowfat soft cheese with herbs and garlic

4 scallions, chopped finely

a few drops of Tabasco sauce

salt and pepper, to taste

potato skins with guacamole

Bake the potatoes in a preheated oven at 400°F/200°C for 1 1/4 hours. Remove from the oven and allow to cool for 30 minutes. Reset the oven to 425°F/220°C.

Halve the potatoes lengthwise and scoop out 2 tablespoons of the flesh. Place the skins on a cookie sheet and brush the flesh side lightly with oil. Sprinkle with salt and pepper. Bake for an additional 25 minutes until golden and crisp.

To make the guacamole dip, mash the avocado with the lemon juice. Add the remaining ingredients and mix. Transfer to a serving bowl.

Drain the potato skins on paper towels and transfer to a warmed serving platter. Serve hot with the guacamole dip.

serves 4

1 lb/450 g potatoes, peeled

2 tbsp corn oil

salt and pepper

ketchup and mayonnaise,
to serve (optional)

homemade oven fries

Preheat the oven to 400°F/200°C.

Cut the potatoes into thick, even-size fries. Rinse them under cold running water and then dry well on a clean dish towel. Put in a bowl, add the oil, and toss together until thoroughly coated.

Spread the fries on a baking sheet and cook in the preheated oven for 40–45 minutes, turning once, until golden. Add salt and pepper to taste and serve hot with ketchup and mayonnaise, if desired.

makes about 9 oz/250 g

3 tbsp sunflower oil

1/3 cup popcorn kernels

2 tbsp butter

1/3 cup brown sugar

2 tbsp corn syrup

1 tbsp milk

1/3 cup semisweet chocolate chips

chocolate popcorn

Preheat the oven to 300°F/150°C. Heat the oil in a large, heavy-bottom pan. Add the popcorn kernels, cover the pan, and cook, shaking the pan vigorously and frequently, for about 2 minutes, until the popping stops. Turn into a large bowl.

Put the butter, sugar, corn syrup, and milk in a pan and heat gently until the butter has melted. Bring to a boil, without stirring, and boil for 2 minutes. Remove from the heat, add the chocolate chips, and stir until melted.

Pour the chocolate mixture over the popcorn and toss together until evenly coated. Spread the mixture onto a large cookie sheet.

Bake the popcorn in the oven for about 15 minutes, until crisp. Let cool before serving.

Lighter Bites

serves 4

4 tenderloin steaks, about
4 oz/115 g each, fat discarded

2 tbsp red wine vinegar

2 tbsp orange juice

2 tsp prepared English mustard

2 eggs

6 oz/175 g baby new potatoes

4 oz/115 g green beans,
trimmed

6 oz/175 g mixed salad
greens, such as baby spinach,
arugula, and mizuna

1 yellow bell pepper, seeded,
peeled, and cut into strips

6 oz/175 g cherry tomatoes,
halved

black olives, pitted (optional)

2 tsp extra virgin olive oil

pepper

warm beef niçoise

Place the steaks in a shallow dish. Blend the vinegar with
1 tablespoon of the orange juice and 1 teaspoon of the mustard.
Pour over the steaks, cover, then let stand in the refrigerator for
at least 30 minutes. Turn over halfway through the marinating time.

Place the eggs in a pan and cover with cold water. Bring to a
boil, then reduce the heat to a simmer and cook for 10 minutes.
Remove and plunge the eggs into cold water. Once cold, shell
and set aside.

Meanwhile, place the potatoes in a pan and cover with cold
water. Bring to a boil, then cover and let simmer for 15 minutes,
or until tender when pierced with a fork. Drain and set aside.

Bring a pan of water to a boil. Add the beans, then cover and
let simmer for 5–8 minutes, or until tender. Drain, then plunge
into cold water. Drain again and set aside. Meanwhile, arrange
the potatoes and beans on top of the salad greens together with
the bell pepper, cherry tomatoes, and olives, if using. Chop the
reserved hard-cooked eggs into wedges and scatter over the
salad. Blend the remaining orange juice and mustard with the
olive oil, season to taste with pepper and reserve.

Heat a stovetop grill pan until smoking. Drain the steaks and
cook for 3–5 minutes on each side or according to personal
preference. Slice the steaks and arrange on top of the salad, then
pour over the dressing and serve.

serves 4

8 oz/225 g baby asparagus spears

1 small or 1/2 medium-size canteloupe melon

2 oz/55 g Parma ham, thinly sliced

51/2 oz/150 g bag of mixed salad greens, such as herb salad with arugula

5/8 cup fresh raspberries

1 tbsp freshly shaved Parmesan cheese

1 tbsp balsamic vinegar

2 tbsp raspberry vinegar

2 tbsp orange juice

parma ham with melon & asparagus

Trim the asparagus, cutting in half if very long. Cook in lightly boiling water over medium heat for 5 minutes, or until tender. Drain and plunge into cold water, then drain again and set aside.

Cut the melon in half and scoop out the seeds. Cut into small wedges and cut away the rind. Separate the Parma ham and cut the slices in half, then wrap around the melon wedges.

Arrange the salad greens on a large serving platter and place the melon wedges on top together with the asparagus spears.

Scatter over the raspberries and Parmesan shavings. Place the vinegars and orange juice in a screw-top jar and shake until blended. Pour over the salad and serve.

serves 4

4 skinless, boneless chicken breasts, about 5 oz/140 g each

4 tsp Cajun seasoning

2 tsp corn oil

1 ripe mango, peeled, seeded, and cut into thick slices

7 oz/200 g mixed salad greens

1 red onion, thinly sliced and cut in half

6 oz/175 g cooked beets, diced

3 oz/85 g radishes, sliced

1/2 cup walnut halves

4 tbsp walnut oil

1–2 tsp Dijon mustard

1 tbsp lemon juice

salt and pepper

2 tbsp sesame seeds

cajun chicken salad

Make 3 diagonal slashes across each chicken breast. Put the chicken into a shallow dish and sprinkle all over with the Cajun seasoning. Cover and let chill for at least 30 minutes.

When ready to cook, brush a stove-top grill pan with the corn oil. Heat over high heat until very hot and a few drops of water sprinkled into the pan sizzle immediately. Add the chicken and cook for 7–8 minutes on each side, or until thoroughly cooked. If still slightly pink in the center, cook a little longer. Remove the chicken and set aside.

Add the mango slices to the pan and cook for 2 minutes on each side. Remove and set aside.

Meanwhile, arrange the salad greens in a salad bowl and sprinkle over the onion, beets, radishes, and walnut halves.

Put the walnut oil, mustard, lemon juice, and salt and pepper to taste in a screw-top jar and shake until well blended. Pour over the salad and sprinkle with the sesame seeds.

Add the mango and chicken to the salad bowl and serve immediately.

serves 4

4 oz/115 g cherry or baby plum tomatoes

several lettuce leaves

4 ripe tomatoes, coarsely chopped

4^1/$_2$ oz/125 g smoked salmon

7 oz/200 g large cooked shrimp, thawed if frozen

1 tbsp Dijon mustard

2 tsp superfine sugar

2 tsp red wine vinegar

2 tbsp medium olive oil

few fresh dill sprigs

pepper

warmed rolls or ciabatta bread

tomato, salmon & shrimp salad

Halve most of the cherry tomatoes. Place the lettuce leaves around the edge of a shallow bowl and add all the tomatoes and cherry tomatoes. Using scissors, snip the smoked salmon into strips and sprinkle over the tomatoes, then add the shrimp.

Mix the mustard, sugar, vinegar, and oil together in a small bowl, then tear most of the dill sprigs into it. Mix well and pour over the salad. Toss well to coat the salad with the dressing. Snip the remaining dill over the top and season to taste with pepper.

Serve the salad with warmed rolls or ciabatta bread.

serves 4

24 raw jumbo shrimp,
thawed if frozen

1 bay leaf

2 tbsp lime juice

1 tsp hot paprika

salt and pepper

2 shallots, coarsely chopped

1 garlic clove, coarsely
chopped

1 tbsp light soy sauce

1 tbsp peanuts

1 tbsp unsweetened dried
coconut

1/2 red bell pepper, seeded
and chopped

7 oz/200 g canned tomatoes

sunflower oil, for brushing

lime wedges, to garnish

spicy shrimp

Pull the heads off the shrimp and peel off the shells. Place the heads, shells, and bay leaf in a pan and add enough cold water to cover. Bring to a boil, then lower the heat, and simmer for 30 minutes.

Meanwhile, using a sharp knife, cut along the back of each shrimp. Remove the dark vein with the point of the knife. Place the shrimp in a nonmetallic dish and sprinkle with the lime juice and paprika. Season with salt and pepper and toss well to coat. Cover with plastic wrap and let marinate in the refrigerator.

Put the shallots, garlic, soy sauce, peanuts, coconut, and bell pepper in a food processor. Drain the tomatoes, reserving 5 tablespoons of the can juice. Add the tomatoes and the reserved can juice to the food processor. Process until smooth. Scrape the mixture into a pan.

When the shellfish stock is ready, strain it into a pitcher, pour it into the pan, and bring the mixture to a boil, stirring occasionally. Lower the heat and simmer for 25–30 minutes until thickened.

Brush a grill pan with oil and preheat. Remove the shrimp from the refrigerator and thread them loosely onto skewers to make handling them easier. When the grill is hot, add the shrimp, and cook for 2 minutes, or until they have changed color and are cooked through.

Transfer the shrimp to a serving dish—with or without the skewers—and garnish with lime wedges. Pour the dipping sauce into a bowl and serve with the shrimp.

serves 4

olive oil, for brushing and drizzling

1 red bell pepper, halved and seeded

1 orange bell pepper, halved and seeded

4 thick slices baguette or ciabatta

1 fennel bulb, sliced

1 red onion, sliced

2 zucchini, sliced diagonally

2 garlic cloves, halved

1 tomato, halved

salt and pepper

fresh sage leaves, to garnish

mixed vegetable bruschetta

Brush a grill pan with oil and preheat. Cut each bell pepper half lengthwise into 4 strips. Toast the bread slices on both sides in a toaster or under a broiler.

When the grill is hot add the bell peppers and fennel and cook for 4 minutes, then add the onion and zucchini, and cook for 5 minutes more until all the vegetables are tender but still with a slight "bite." If necessary, cook the vegetables in 2 batches, as they should be placed on the grill in a single layer.

Meanwhile, rub the garlic halves over the toasts, then rub them with the tomato halves. Place on warm plates. Pile the grilled vegetables on top of the toasts, drizzle with olive oil, and season with salt and pepper. Garnish with sage leaves and serve warm.

serves 4

10 oz/280 g buffalo mozzarella,
drained and sliced thinly

8 plum tomatoes, sliced

salt and pepper

20 fresh basil leaves

4 fl oz/125 ml extra virgin
olive oil

three-color salad

Arrange the cheese and tomato slices on 4 individual serving plates and season to taste with salt. Set aside in a cool place for 30 minutes.

Sprinkle the basil leaves over the salad and drizzle with the olive oil. Season with pepper and serve immediately.

serves 6

1 lb/450 g red cabbage

1 apple

4 tbsp orange juice

1 large carrot, peeled and grated

1 red onion, peeled and cut into tiny wedges

6 oz/175 g cherry tomatoes, halved

3-inch/7.5-cm piece cucumber, peeled if preferred, and diced

1/3 cup fresh dates, pitted and chopped

1 tbsp extra virgin olive oil

1 tbsp chopped fresh flat-leaf parsley

pepper

red cabbage slaw

Discard the outer leaves and hard central core from the cabbage and shred finely. Wash thoroughly in plenty of cold water, then shake dry and place in a salad bowl.

Core the apple and chop, toss in 1 tablespoon of the orange juice, then add to the salad bowl together with the carrot, onion, tomatoes, cucumber, and dates.

Place the remaining orange juice in a screw-top jar, add the oil, parsley, and pepper and shake until blended. Pour the dressing over the salad and toss lightly, then serve.

serves 4–6

1 cup mixed soft fruits, such as blueberries, raspberries, and pitted fresh cherries

1^1/$_2$–2 tbsp Cointreau or orange flower water

1^1/$_8$ cups mascarpone cheese

scant 1 cup sour cream

2–3 tbsp brown sugar

cheat's crème brûlée

Prepare the fruit, if necessary, and lightly rinse, then place in the bases of 4–6 x ^{2}/$_3$-cup ramekins. Sprinkle the fruit with the Cointreau or orange flower water.

Cream the mascarpone cheese in a bowl until soft, then gradually beat in the sour cream.

Spoon the cheese mixture over the fruit, smoothing the surface and ensuring that the tops are level. Let chill in the refrigerator for at least 2 hours.

Sprinkle the tops with the sugar. Using a chef's blowtorch, broil the tops until caramelized (about 2–3 minutes). Alternatively, cook under a preheated broiler, turning the dishes, for 3–4 minutes, or until the tops are lightly caramelized all over.

Serve at once or let chill in the refrigerator for 15–20 minutes before serving.

makes 4

a selection of fruit, such as apricots, peaches, figs, strawberries, mangoes, pineapple, bananas, dates, and papaya, prepared and cut into chunks

maple syrup

1³/4 oz/50 g semisweet chocolate (minimum 70% cocoa solids), broken into chunks

fruit skewers

Soak 4 bamboo skewers in water for at least 20 minutes.

Preheat the broiler to high and line the broiler pan with foil. Thread alternate pieces of fruit onto each skewer. Brush the fruit with a little maple syrup.

Put the chocolate in a heatproof bowl, set the bowl over a pan of barely simmering water, and heat until it is melted.

Meanwhile, cook the skewers under the preheated broiler for 3 minutes, or until caramelized. Serve drizzled with a little of the melted chocolate.

Food on the Go

serves 4

1 tbsp butter

1/2 red onion, minced

1 leek, chopped

1 garlic clove, crushed

1 carrot, peeled and grated

1 potato, peeled and grated

1 1/4 cups vegetable stock

1 lb 2 oz/500 g ripe tomatoes, peeled, seeded, and chopped

1 tbsp tomato paste

sea salt and pepper

2/3 cup whole milk

snipped chives, to garnish (optional)

slices of seeded bread, to serve

creamy tomato soup

Melt the butter in a large pan over low heat and cook the onion, leek, and garlic for 10 minutes, or until very soft but not browned.

Add the carrot and potato and cook for 5 minutes. Add the stock and bring up to the simmering point.

Add the tomatoes and tomato paste and season to taste with salt and pepper. Let simmer for 15 minutes until the vegetables are very soft. Add the milk and warm through, then transfer the soup to a blender or food processor and process until very smooth. You can pass the soup through a strainer at this stage, if you like.

Return the soup to the rinsed-out pan and reheat gently. Garnish the soup with snipped chives, if desired, and serve with slices of seeded bread.

serves 4

14 oz/400g canned refried beans

8 flour tortillas

1³/4 cups grated Cheddar cheese

1 onion, chopped

¹/2 bunch fresh cilantro leaves, chopped, plus extra leaves to garnish

for the tomato salsa

6–8 ripe tomatoes, finely chopped

about 3¹/2 fl oz/100 ml tomato juice

3–4 garlic cloves, finely chopped

¹/2 bunch fresh cilantro leaves, coarsely chopped

pinch of sugar

3–4 fresh green chiles, seeded and finely chopped

¹/2–1 tsp ground cumin

3–4 scallions, finely chopped

salt

cheese & bean quesadillas

To make the tomato salsa, stir all the ingredients together in a bowl and season with salt to taste. Cover with plastic wrap and chill in the refrigerator until required.

Place the beans in a small pan and set over low heat to warm through.

Meanwhile, make the tortillas pliable by warming them gently in a lightly greased nonstick skillet.

Remove the tortillas from the skillet and quickly spread with a layer of warm beans. Top each tortilla with grated cheese, onion, fresh cilantro, and a spoonful of salsa. Roll up tightly.

Just before serving, heat the nonstick skillet over medium heat, sprinkling lightly with a couple of drops of water. Add the tortilla rolls, cover the skillet, and heat through until the cheese melts. Allow to brown lightly, if desired.

Remove the tortilla rolls from the skillet and slice each roll, on the diagonal, into about 4 bite-size pieces. Serve the quesadillas hot or cold, garnished with cilantro leaves.

serves 4

4 ciabatta rolls

2 tbsp olive oil

1 garlic clove, crushed

for the filling

1 red bell pepper

1 green bell pepper

1 yellow bell pepper

4 radishes, sliced

1 bunch of watercress

1/2 cup cream cheese

ciabatta rolls

Slice the ciabatta rolls in half. Heat the olive oil and garlic in a pan. Brush the garlic and oil mixture over the cut surfaces of the rolls and set aside.

Halve and seed the bell peppers and place, skin-side up, on a broiler rack. Cook under a preheated hot broiler for 8–10 minutes until just beginning to char. Remove the bell peppers from the broiler and place in a plastic bag. When cool enough to handle, peel and slice thinly.

Arrange the radish slices on 1 half of each roll with a few watercress leaves. Spoon the cream cheese on top. Pile the roasted bell peppers on top of the cream cheese and top with the other half of the roll. Serve immediately.

serves 4

5 oz/140 g butter

1 onion, finely chopped

1 garlic clove, finely chopped

9 oz/250 g chicken livers

salt and pepper

1/2 tsp Dijon mustard

2 tbsp brandy (optional)

brown toast strips, to serve

for the clarified butter

4 oz/115 g lightly salted butter

chicken liver pâté

Melt half the butter in a large skillet over medium heat and cook the onion for 3–4 minutes until soft and transparent. Add the garlic and continue to cook for an additional 2 minutes.

Check the chicken livers and remove any discolored parts using a pair of kitchen scissors. Add the livers to the skillet and cook over a fairly high heat for 5–6 minutes until they are brown in color. Season well with salt and pepper and add the mustard and brandy, if using.

Process the pâté in a blender or food processor until smooth. Add the remaining butter cut into small pieces and process again until creamy.

Press the pâté into a serving dish or 4 small ramekins, smooth over the surface and cover with plastic wrap. If the pâté is to be kept for more than 2 days, you could cover the surface with a little clarified butter. In a clean saucepan, heat the butter until it melts, then continue heating for a few moments until it stops bubbling. Allow the sediment to settle and carefully pour the clarified butter over the pâté.

Chill in the refrigerator until ready to serve, accompanied by toast strips.

serves 4

6 oz/175 g canned chickpeas

1/2 cup tahini

2 garlic cloves

1/2 cup lemon juice

salt

2–3 tbsp water

1 tbsp olive oil

1 tbsp chopped fresh parsley

pinch of cayenne pepper

for the crudités

selection of vegetables, including carrots, cauliflower, and celery

hummus with crudités

Drain and rinse the chickpeas. Place them in a blender or food processor with the tahini, garlic, and lemon juice. Season to taste with salt. Process, gradually adding the water, until smooth and creamy.

Scrape the chickpea mixture into a serving bowl and make a hollow in the center. Pour the olive oil into the hollow and sprinkle with the chopped fresh parsley and the cayenne.

Slice the raw vegetables into bite-size portions and arrange on a large serving platter. Serve with the hummus.

serves 6

7 oz/200 g new potatoes

1 tbsp olive oil

1 onion, thinly sliced

1 red bell pepper, seeded and thinly sliced

2 tomatoes, peeled, seeded, and chopped

6 large eggs

1 tbsp milk

1¼ oz/35 g Parmesan cheese, finely grated

sea salt and pepper

spanish omelet

Cook the potatoes in a pan of boiling water for 8–12 minutes until tender. Drain and let cool, then slice.

Heat the oil in a 7–8-inch/18–20-cm skillet with a heatproof handle and cook the sliced onion and red bell pepper until soft. Add the tomatoes and cook for an additional minute.

Add the potatoes to the skillet and spread out evenly. Beat the eggs, milk, cheese, and salt and pepper to taste, in a bowl and pour over the potato mixture. Cook for 4–5 minutes until the eggs are set underneath.

Meanwhile, preheat the broiler to high. Place the skillet under the broiler and cook the omelet for an additional 3–4 minutes until the eggs are set.

Leave to cool, then cut into wedges and wrap in foil for a lunch box or spear onto toothpicks for a party snack.

serves 4

scant 1¹/4 cups sushi rice

2 tbsp rice vinegar

1 tsp superfine sugar

¹/2 tsp salt

4 sheets nori

for the fillings

1³/4 oz/50 g smoked salmon

1¹/2-inch/4-cm piece cucumber, peeled, seeded, and cut into short thin sticks

1¹/2 oz/40 g cooked shelled shrimp

1 small avocado, pitted, peeled, thinly sliced, and tossed in lemon juice

to serve

wasabi (Japanese horseradish sauce)

tamari (wheat-free soy sauce)

pink pickled ginger

mixed sushi rolls

Put the rice into a pan and cover with cold water. Bring to a boil, then reduce the heat, cover, and let simmer for 15–20 minutes, or until the rice is tender and the water has been absorbed. Drain if necessary and transfer to a bowl. Mix the vinegar, sugar, and salt together, then, using a spatula, stir well into the rice. Cover with a damp cloth and let cool.

To make the rolls, lay a clean bamboo mat over a cutting board. Lay a sheet of nori, shiny-side down, on the mat. Spread a quarter of the rice mixture over the nori, using wet fingers to press it down evenly, leaving a ¹/2-inch/1-cm margin at the top and bottom.

For smoked salmon and cucumber rolls, lay the salmon over the rice and arrange the cucumber in a line across the center. For the shrimp rolls, lay the shrimp and avocado in a line across the center.

Carefully hold the nearest edge of the mat, then, using the mat as a guide, roll up the nori tightly to make a neat tube of rice enclosing the filling. Seal the uncovered edge with a little water, then roll the sushi off the mat. Repeat to make 3 more rolls—you need 2 salmon and cucumber and 2 shrimp and avocado in total.

Using a wet knife, cut each roll into 8 pieces and stand upright on a platter. Wipe and rinse the knife between cuts to prevent the rice from sticking. Serve the rolls with wasabi, tamari, and pickled ginger.

makes 16

3/4 cup unsalted butter, plus extra for greasing

3 tbsp honey

generous 3/4 cup packed raw brown sugar

3 1/2 oz/100 g smooth peanut butter

2 3/4 cups rolled oats

generous 1/4 cup dried apricots, chopped

2 tbsp sunflower seeds

2 tbsp sesame seeds

sticky fruit oat squares

Preheat the oven to 350°F/180°C. Grease and line an 8 1/2-inch/22-cm square baking pan.

Melt the butter, honey, and sugar in a pan over low heat. When the sugar has melted, add the peanut butter, and stir until all the ingredients are well combined. Add all the remaining ingredients and mix well.

Press the mixture into the prepared pan and bake in the preheated oven for 20 minutes.

Remove from the oven and let cool in the pan, then cut into 16 squares.

makes 10

generous 1 cup white all-purpose flour

scant 3/4 cup whole wheat self-rising flour

1 tbsp oat bran

2 tsp baking powder

1/2 tsp baking soda

pinch of salt

1/4 cup packed raw brown sugar

1 tbsp honey

1 large egg

scant 1 cup buttermilk

11/8 cups fresh blueberries

blueberry bran muffins

Preheat the oven to 350°F/180°C. Line 10 holes of a muffin pan with muffin paper cases.

Mix the flours, bran, baking powder, baking soda, and salt together in a bowl and stir in the sugar. Whisk the honey, egg, and buttermilk together in a pitcher.

Pour the wet ingredients into the dry and stir briefly to combine. Don't overmix—the batter should still be a little lumpy. Fold in the blueberries.

Spoon the batter into the paper cases and bake in the preheated oven for 20 minutes until risen and lightly browned.

Remove the muffins from the oven and let cool in the pan. Serve warm or cold.

makes 1 loaf

unsalted butter, for greasing

scant 1 cup white self-rising flour

scant 3/4 cup whole wheat self-rising flour

pinch of salt

1/2 tsp ground cinnamon

1/2 tsp ground nutmeg

generous 3/4 cup packed raw brown sugar

2 large ripe bananas, peeled

3/4 cup orange juice

2 eggs, beaten

4 tbsp canola oil

honey, sliced banana, and chopped walnuts, to serve

banana loaf

Preheat the oven to 350°F/180°C. Lightly grease and line a 1-lb/450-g loaf pan.

Sift the flours, salt, and the spices into a large bowl. Stir in the sugar.

In a separate bowl, mash the bananas with the orange juice, then stir in the eggs and oil. Pour into the dry ingredients and mix well.

Spoon into the prepared loaf pan and bake in the preheated oven for 1 hour, then test to see if it is cooked by inserting a skewer into the center. If it comes out clean, the loaf is done. If not, bake for an additional 10 minutes and test again.

Remove from the oven and let cool in the pan. Turn the loaf out, slice, and serve with honey, sliced banana, and chopped walnuts.